BRITISH RAILWAYS

PAST and PRESENT

No 42

Map of the area covered by this book.

BRITISH RAILWAYS
PAST and PRESENT

No 42
Essex and East Hertfordshire

Paul Shannon

Past & Present Publishing Ltd

© Paul Shannon 2004

All rights reserved. No part of this publication may be reproduced, stored in a retrieval system or transmitted, in any form or by any means, electronic, mechanical, photocopying, recording or otherwise, without prior permission in writing from Past & Present Publishing Ltd.

First published in 2004

British Library Cataloguing in Publication Data

A catalogue record for this book is available from the British Library.

ISBN 1 85895 193 3

Past & Present Publishing Ltd
The Trundle
Ringstead Road
Great Addington
Kettering
Northants NN14 4BW

Tel/Fax: 01536 330588
email: sales@nostalgiacollection.com
Website: www.nostalgiacollection.com

Printed and bound in Great Britain

WITHAM: The Maldon, Witham & Braintree Railway was promoted in 1845 as a free-standing line, but the Eastern Counties Railway permitted the new company to share its main-line station at Witham, effectively dividing the route into two separate branches – Witham to Maldon and Witham to Braintree – which explains the three-way junction that existed here until 1966. A wealth of railway detail can be seen in this view of Class 'F5' 2-4-2T No 67214 arriving at Witham with a midday train from Maldon on 17 March 1958. The maltings on the right would have been an important source of freight at that time.

Total transformation is evident as First Great Eastern unit No 321316 rolls into Witham with the 1727 from Colchester Town to London Liverpool Street on 15 April 2003. Even the power signal box on the right, commissioned in 1961 as a prelude to electrification, is no longer in use. *Frank Church/PDS*

CONTENTS

Introduction	7
London, Tilbury & Southend Railway	9
Great Eastern line to Colchester	29
Great Eastern branches to the coast	40
Cross-country routes via Braintree, Halstead and Sudbury	65
Suburban branch lines	83
Great Eastern line to Cambridge and branches	91
Great Northern lines	111
Index of locations	128

MARKS TEY: Diesel multiple units came early to many rural lines in Essex. They took over the Marks Tey-Sudbury service in January 1959, including the through trains between Colchester and Cambridge that were still in operation at that time. A Wickham two-car unit awaits departure from Marks Tey on 21 March 1959, forming the 5.20pm from Ipswich to Cambridge.

The Wickham units were not a success, and all five of them had been taken out of service by 1971. Two were sold to Trinidad Railways, two were scrapped, and one was converted into a General Manager's saloon. The last-mentioned set passed into preservation and when this book went to press was undergoing restoration at Butterley with support from the Heritage Lottery Fund. Services on the Sudbury branch, meanwhile, are in the hands of Class 150 'Sprinter' units, leased to First Great Eastern from Anglia Railways. No 150245 waits to form the 0834 Marks Tey to Sudbury train on 14 April 2003. *Michael Mensing/PDS*

INTRODUCTION

The area covered in this book stretches from the busy London suburbs to the quiet backwaters of the Essex/Suffolk border, with railway routes ranging from the prestigious Great Eastern and Great Northern main lines to humble single-track branch lines and cross-country byways.

Until the 1923 Grouping, the Great Eastern Railway was the dominant railway company in the area, but the Great Northern Railway served a sizeable slice of Hertfordshire and the London, Tilbury & Southend Railway (which became part of the Midland Railway in 1912) ran a busy network of lines in South Essex. There were smaller companies, too, including the Colne Valley & Halstead Railway and the Corringham Light Railway, the latter remaining independent right up to its closure in 1952.

The railway system of Essex and East Hertfordshire reached its zenith in the 1930s after the completion of the GNR's Hertford loop and the quadrupling of tracks from Barking to Upminster and from Gidea Park to Shenfield. But the period of relative stability was short. Even before the Second World War the LNER was feeling the effects of road competition on some of its branches, and in 1939 the Woodham Ferrers-Maldon line lost its passenger service. From 1950 onwards, British Railways started the process of rationalisation in earnest, with lesser-used lines closing while the busier routes benefited from resignalling, electrification and overall service improvements.

Among the passenger closures that pre-dated the Beeching Report of 1963 were Hertford-Welwyn Garden City, Braintree-Bishop's Stortford, Chappel-Haverhill (Colne Valley) and the Light Railway branches to Tollesbury and Thaxted, while the Report itself hastened the demise of branches to Maldon, Brightlingsea and Buntingford, as well as Audley End-Bartlow and the cross-country link from Sudbury to Shelford. The Ongar branch finally closed in 1994 after surviving for more than three decades as an anomalous extension of the Central Line.

Dieselisation came early to the GER and LT&SR networks, with steam virtually eliminated by the early 1960s. Many of the suburban routes went straight from steam to electric, as British Railways – or London Transport in the case of the Epping branch – opted for what would nowadays be called 'total route modernisation'. That explains why most of the 'past' photographs in this book were taken in 1962 or earlier – enthusiasts tended to give the area a wide berth while there was still working steam elsewhere.

The relentless spread of commuter settlement is a recurring theme in this book, with more people choosing to live further away from London to benefit from lower house prices and a perceived improvement in quality of life. The single-track branches to Witham and Southminster survived long enough to benefit from electrification, extended platforms and regular-interval through trains to and from London – a far cry from their rural origins. But the growth of long-distance commuting came too late to save the Buntingford and Maldon branches.

In the 1990s proposals were made to reinstate part or all of two former railway routes: Braintree-Bishop's Stortford and Sudbury-Cambridge. The aim of the first proposal was to provide a rail link to Stansted Airport from the east, using new alignments as well as part of the former trackbed. Unfortunately, the idea has so far failed to attract Government support. On the Sudbury-Cambridge route, a pre-feasibility study in 1999 concluded that reinstatement of the Haverhill-Cambridge section would offer good value for money. Again, however, nothing will happen unless there is a significant change in Government policy.

Rail freight in Essex and East Hertfordshire has become more specialised and polarised, as it has throughout the British network. The main lines to Colchester, Cambridge and

Peterborough still carry their share of through traffic, but the number of active freight terminals in the area has declined even within the last ten years. The biggest concentration of activity is found on the former LT&S line between Barking and Tilbury, while a number of formerly busy locations such as Thames Haven and Harwich are disappointingly quiet. Proposals to build a deep-water container port at Thames Haven may yet bring about a revival on that part of the network.

The preservation movement keeps Steam Age memories alive at the East Anglian Railway Museum, located beside Chappel & Wakes Colne station, and at the Colne Valley Railway, near Sible & Castle Hedingham. Another interesting collection of historic railway items can be seen at Mangapps Railway Museum, near Burnham-on-Crouch. Meanwhile, the return of train services to the Ongar branch is still eagerly awaited, after a lengthy and costly period of negotiations between several interested parties.

Retracing the footsteps of photographers 40 or 50 years ago was, as always, a fascinating experience. Some potentially good material had to be rejected because the vantage point was no longer accessible, often because of the closure of footpaths or the removal of bridges. Many stretches of closed railway are out of bounds, but the Flitch Way path near Dunmow was a refreshing find and some stretches of the Maldon branch are still walkable. It is always pleasing to see examples of railway architecture being cared for long after the railway has gone, such as at Maldon, Braughing and Bartlow.

On those lines still open today, the photographer faces more challenges today than in the days of steam. Lineside views 'looking over the fence' are generally impossible today because of dense undergrowth and/or the erection of high-security fencing – the latter spreading fast in 2003 at a reputed cost of up to £60,000 a mile. At stations, the opportunities for photography have become more restricted in recent years, but at some locations – especially on routes operated by First Great Eastern – I found the railway staff interested and helpful.

The process of change is, of course, ongoing. I have included a number of nostalgic views from the 1980s, and some of the 'present' scenes in this book will soon become history – such as the 'second generation' Class 312 units on Great Eastern lines, which are due for withdrawal in 2004. The re-franchising process currently under way in East Anglia will doubtless produce another new rolling-stock livery, while the Channel Tunnel Rail Link will soon transform the railway scene between Dagenham and Purfleet.

I am grateful to all the photographers and copyright holders who allowed me to use their material, particularly to Richard Casserley and David Holmes for help with identifying locomotives and providing additional caption details.

Paul Shannon, Chester

BIBLIOGRAPHY

ABC British Railways Locomotives, combined volumes: various years (Ian Allan)
ABC London Underground *by John Glover* (Ian Allan)
ABC Railway Freight Operations *by Paul Shannon* (Ian Allan)
British Marshalling Yards *by Michael Rhodes* (OPC)
Freight Only Yearbook Nos 1 and 2 *by Michael Rhodes and Paul Shannon* (Silver Link Publishing)
Passengers No More *by Gerald Daniels and L. A. Dench* (Ian Allan)

A Pictorial Survey of Railway Signalling *by D. Allen and C. J. Woolstenholmes* (OPC)
Railway Correspondence and Travel Society Locomotive Stock Books: 1963, 1966 and 1969
A Regional History of the Railways of Great Britain: Volume 3 Greater London *by H. P. White* (David & Charles)
A Regional History of the Railways of Great Britain: Volume 5 Eastern Counties *by David St John Thomas* (David & Charles)

The Thames Haven Railway *by Peter Kay*
Today's Railways Review of the Year: Volumes 1, 2, 3 and 4 (Platform Five Publishing)

Back issues of:
Branch Line News
British Railways Illustrated
Hertfordshire Countryside
Modern Railways
Rail
Railway Magazine
The Railway Observer
Railway World

The London, Tilbury & Southend Railway

The London, Tilbury & Southend Railway was launched in 1854 with the opening of its 17-mile line from Forest Gate Junction, east of Stratford, to the port of Tilbury. That route became the backbone of a busy network serving East London and South Essex, all of which are still in use today.

Despite its proximity to the GER, the LT&SR was absorbed by the Midland Railway in 1912 and became part of the LMS in 1923. Electrification had been proposed by the Midland Railway to cope with the increasing commuter traffic between Southend and London, but in the event steam working was to continue until 1962.

Today, passenger operations on the LT&SR system are largely self-contained. Commuters have recently benefited from new Class 357 rolling-stock, as well as a more reliable signalling system. The line as far as Tilbury also carries large quantities of freight, including deep-sea and European container traffic, aggregates, paper and automotive traffic.

BARKING station increased in importance with the opening of the direct Barking-Upminster-Pitsea line in 1888 and the arrival of the District Line from Whitechapel in 1902. Major remodelling took place in the 1930s, when the Barking-Upminster section was quadrupled and five new intermediate stations were opened. On 14 October 1957 BR Class '4MT' 2-6-4T No 80132 arrives at Barking with the 2.40pm from Fenchurch Street to Tilbury.

Further remodelling took place from 1959 onwards in readiness for electrification. Better interchange facilities for passengers were provided at Barking, together with burrowing and flying junctions to minimise conflicting movements. With one of the flyovers just visible in the distance, a District Line train of 'D' stock departs for central London on 17 April 2003. *H. C. Casserley/PDS*

UPMINSTER: On 11 June 1938, shortly after quadruple track had been extended from Barking, Stanier three-cylinder Class '4MT' 2-6-4T No 2510 enters Upminster station with the 5.18pm from Shoeburyness. This busy junction provided interchange between the Barking-Pitsea and Romford-Grays lines as well as with the District Line of the London Underground.

Sixty-five years later Upminster is still a busy junction, but the track layout, signalling and rolling-stock have changed substantially. The connection between London Underground and BR/Network Rail lines has been removed, and the former goods yard is now a car park. Unit No 357015 calls with the 1120 Southend Central to Fenchurch Street service on 19 April 2003. *H. C. Casserley/PDS*

OCKENDON: The link between Upminster and Grays opened in 1892, offering an alternative route between London and Tilbury as well as catering for local traffic. Calling at the intermediate station of Ockendon on 20 May 1957 are auto-trains for Upminster and Grays, powered by Class 'N7' 0-6-2T No 69691 and Class 'C12' 4-4-2T No 67363 respectively. The latter locomotive was one of the few survivors of a class introduced in 1898.

Today, high-security fencing and cameras are an unattractive, but sadly necessary, feature of Ockendon station. The line supports a half-hourly off-peak service between London Fenchurch Street and Southend Central, with extra trains in the rush hour. Unit No 357228 calls with the 1550 departure from Fenchurch Street on 18 April 2003. *Frank Church/PDS*

RIPPLE LANE became an important freight centre in the late 1950s, when British Railways built a new hump marshalling yard to serve London Docks and other goods terminals on North Thamesside. The yard was the first of its type to be placed between the two running lines, an arrangement that still exists today, even though very little of the yard remains in use. On 4 July 1989, shortly after the wiring up of the North London line had made it possible for electric locomotives to reach North Thamesside, Class 86 locomotives Nos 86427 and 86406 pass Ripple Lane with empty Freightliner flats for Tilbury. The vast shed in the background was still in use as a general distribution terminal, handling mainly steel and imported goods.

In 1992 new warehousing was erected on the site of Ripple Lane freight terminal to handle trainloads of imported paper; this traffic still operates today on behalf of Stora Enso. With pilot loco No 08635 resting between duties, Class 66 No 66042 heads east on the main line with 6L35, the 1004 Enterprise service from Wembley to Purfleet, on 24 August 2001. *Both PDS*

DAGENHAM DOCK: The Ford Motor Company established its Dagenham works in the 1930s, transforming an area of wasteland into a busy industrial location. This photograph, dated 6 June 1959, offers glimpses of the various types of freight traffic generated by Ford on both sides of the line, as BR Class '4MT' 2-6-4T No 80071 enters Dagenham Dock station with the 11.55am service from Tilbury to Fenchurch Street.

The masts and wires of electrification were installed not long after the date of the 'past' picture, but Dagenham Dock signal box remained in use until 1996. Unit No 357210 approaches the station with the 1447 from Grays to Fenchurch Street on 17 April 2003. Although Ford no longer manufactures cars at Dagenham, the freight sidings remain in use for automotive components and imported vehicles, together with non-automotive flows of aggregates and waste. *H. C. Casserley/PDS*

RAINHAM: The Midland Railway origin of Rainham box is unmistakeable, as Class 37 No 37706 passes with a trip working from Thames Haven to Ripple Lane on 17 February 1989. This was one of a small number of trains that catered at that time for wagonload traffic from the Thames Haven refineries, in this case bitumen for Frome.

The searchlight signal has been replaced by the standard four-aspect type and the signal box has given way to centralised control from Upminster panel. Construction work for the Channel Tunnel Rail Link is under way in the 'present' photograph dated 17 April 2003. *Both PDS*

PURFLEET: The level crossing gates are receiving a new coat of paint as Class '4MT' 2-6-4T No 80136 approaches Purfleet station with a London-bound train on 23 May 1959. The skyline is dominated by the cranes of Purfleet coal wharves and, on the other side of the Thames, the chimneys of Littlebrook power station. Parked just behind the signal box appears to be a diesel shunter.

On 18 April 2003 unit No 357020 rounds the curve at Purfleet with the 1702 departure from Grays to Barking. Most of the sidings in the 'past' photograph have gone, although half a mile or so towards Tilbury there is still plenty of rail freight activity. The industrial backdrop has also changed, with the Queen Elizabeth II road bridge now a prominent feature. No 80136 was purchased by the Class 4 Preservation Trust and is on loan to the West Somerset Railway at the time of writing. *Frank Church/PDS*

TILBURY RIVERSIDE (1): The railway terminus at Tilbury was built primarily to connect with the Gravesend ferry service. Later, the pier attracted pleasure steamers and ocean liner traffic, with the railway providing special boat trains as required. The station was rebuilt in 1930 and renamed Tilbury Riverside six years later. On 15 February 1958 Class '4F' 0-6-0 No 44029 rounds the west curve into Riverside with a P&O boat train from St Pancras.

The ocean liner traffic declined as air travel became established in the early 1960s, and the last St Pancras boat train ran in 1963. The Gravesend ferry traffic kept Riverside in business, but this too declined after the opening of the Dartford Tunnel and the station eventually closed in November 1992. The site then became a freight terminal, initially for Channel Tunnel traffic, then as an overspill for Tilbury Freightliner terminal. Class 47 No 47234 sets out with the 1754 Freightliner working to Cardiff Pengam on 29 July 1999. *Frank Church/PDS*

TILBURY RIVERSIDE (2): Class 302 unit No 270 stands at the faded Riverside terminus on 18 April 1984. By this time the flow of rail passengers had diminished to a trickle, and the station had just lost its platform canopies to save the cost of repairs.

It came as no surprise when BR posted closure notices for Tilbury Riverside in 1989. Eventually, after some local resistance, the last train ran in November 1992. The freight terminal that became established on the site got off to a disappointing start, with Channel Tunnel traffic failing to materialise. However, Freightliner brought some regular business and, in January 2002, Victa Railfreight became the terminal operator, handling intermodal traffic for EWS as well as Freightliner. Meanwhile, the local train-operating company has continued to provide Gravesend passengers with a minibus connection between Tilbury Town station and Riverside ferry terminal. The 'present' picture is dated 22 October 2002. *Both PDS*

TILBURY EAST JUNCTION: The LT&SR engine shed lay in the triangle of lines at the north end of Riverside station. Also within the triangle were three rows of railwaymen's cottages. The east end of the shed is pictured on 19 July 1959, with ex-Midland Railway 0-6-0 No 43934 rounding the east curve and ex-LMS 0-6-0 No 44581 waiting on the north curve with the Orient Line boat train. With electrification looming, this scene would change completely within a couple of years.

On 18 April 2003 the area once occupied by the engine shed awaits commercial development, together with the disused trackbed of the east curve. The double-track north curve continues to be used by the half-hourly passenger service between Fenchurch Street and Southend Central. *Frank Church/PDS*

THAMES HAVEN BRANCH: The 3¾-mile branch to Thames Haven was primarily a freight railway, but from 1923 until 1958 it carried a daily workmen's train to and from Thames Haven. Four intermediate halts were provided on the branch, all with ground-level 'platforms' and small timber shelters. Mayes Crossing Halt is pictured here in the spring of 1955, with ex-LT&SR 0-6-0T No 41991 hauling the Saturday lunchtime service from Thames Haven.

After the withdrawal of the workmen's trains, all traces of the halts quickly disappeared, but the branch then enjoyed its busiest period with block oil trains from the two refineries at Thames Haven. However, the oil traffic has declined sharply in recent years: the Shell refinery closed to rail in 1993 and the Mobil refinery only produces four trains a week at the time of writing. The site of Mayes Crossing is pictured on 18 April 2003. *Frank Church/PDS*

CORRINGHAM LIGHT RAILWAY (1): Built mainly to carry workers from the villages of Corringham and Fobbing to the Kynochs explosive works at Kynochtown, near Thames Haven, the 2½-mile Corringham Light Railway opened as an independent concern in 1901. This postcard view shows the Corringham terminus in its early years.

The line carried increased business during the First World War, but the building of a new road then took away much of its traffic, and by the end of the Second World War most potential passengers were travelling by bus. The last train ran on 1 March 1952 and the track was lifted shortly afterwards. Since then, the former station area at Corringham has been transformed into a peaceful garden, as pictured on 18 April 2003. A house just visible between the trees provides a definite link between the two photographs. *Tom Middlemass collection/PDS*

CORRINGHAM LIGHT RAILWAY (2): The railway's Kynochtown terminus was renamed Coryton in 1921 when the explosives works and its associated village were sold to Cory Bros Ltd for development as an oil refinery. Pictured at Coryton on 17 May 1947 is an 0-6-0 saddle-tank (works number 1771) built by the Avonside Engine Company in 1917, coupled to the standard passenger accommodation of the day, an ex-LT&SR coach dating back to 1876, without heat, light, brakes, nor even a guard's compartment!

After the withdrawal of passenger services in 1952, the eastern end of the former Light Railway became busy with oil trains from Coryton refinery, using a connection with the Thames Haven branch. Meanwhile the village of Coryton was depopulated in 1970 to permit expansion of the oil refinery. The refinery sidings are pictured on 18 April 2003, with bitumen tanks for Llandarcy awaiting transfer to the EWS yard at Thames Haven. *H. C. Casserley/PDS*

STANFORD-LE-HOPE: The Class 302 electric units introduced with the LT&SR electrification scheme in 1961 remained in use until the 1990s. With the Midland Railway-style signal box and 1950s searchlight signal adding a period flavour, Nos 251 and 246 depart from Stanford-le-Hope with the 0920 London Fenchurch Street-Southend Central service on 18 April 1984. The signal box was to close in the following year, with the crossing placed under CCTV surveillance from Pitsea.

The Class 302s gave way to Class 310 units displaced from the London Midland Region and to Class 312s from Great Eastern lines. Between 1999 and 2002 they in turn were replaced by a fleet of 74 brand-new Class 357 units, bringing to an end the use of slam-door stock on LT&SR routes. Unit No 357036 forms the 0850 Fenchurch Street-Southend train on 18 April 2003. *Both PDS*

PITSEA became a junction with the opening of the direct line from Barking via Upminster in 1888, having previously been a minor intermediate station on the Tilbury to Southend line. With electrification works only a few years away, ex-LMS Fowler Class '4F' 0-6-0 No 44442 enters Pitsea with a Southend excursion on 23 June 1957.

No 44442 was withdrawn from stock in 1963, while a few other members of the class – a post-Grouping development of a Midland Railway design – remained in service until 1966. Meanwhile, steam disappeared from LT&SR lines and, with the run-down of pick-up goods traffic, the appearance of any kind of locomotive on this stretch of the LT&SR became a rarity. Unit No 357222 forms the 0940 service from Fenchurch Street to Shoeburyness on 18 April 2003. *Frank Church/PDS*

LEIGH-ON-SEA: The opening of the LT&SR to Shoeburyness contributed to a massive rise in the population of Southend, from just over 2,000 inhabitants in 1851 to more than 70,000 in 1911. The small fishing port of Leigh-on-Sea was soon engulfed by housing development, eventually stretching all the way to Shoeburyness. The original Leigh-on-Sea station became too cramped for its growing traffic and was closed in 1933 in favour of a new facility half a mile to the west. However, the level crossing at the old station site was still in use when this photograph was taken on 3 August 1958. The former station building on the site of the down platform is visible on the right.

Today it is hard to believe that a level crossing existed here. The view from the relocated footbridge on 18 April 2003 shows unit No 357002 forming the 1050 service from Fenchurch Street to Southend. *Frank Church/PDS*

CHALKWELL: The LMS introduced brand-new Stanier three-cylinder 2-6-4T locomotives on the LT&SR lines in 1934, together with improved carriage stock to cater for the booming commuter traffic, and all 37 members of the class were still allocated to Shoeburyness shed in 1961. No 42518 calls at Chalkwell station with a London-bound train on 23 July of that year.

The changes at Chalkwell station in the last 42 years have been subtle rather than dramatic. The station never had any goods facilities. Unit No 357036 calls with the 1320 service from Southend Central to London Fenchurch Street on 18 April 2003. *Stephen Summerson/PDS*

SOUTHEND CENTRAL became the terminus of the LT&SR in 1856 and remained so until the extension to Shoeburyness opened in 1884. The station layout was enlarged in 1899, with six platform faces catering for regular trains to and from Fenchurch Street and St Pancras as well as summertime excursions. This view, looking towards Shoeburyness, is dated 19 March 1955.

Further alterations took place with electrification, including the replacement of the 1899 signal box by a modern structure. However, that has also since disappeared, with the whole line now coming under the control of Upminster panel. The remaining two island platforms have been lengthened, and the goods yard on the north side of the line has long since been redeveloped. A Class 357 unit waits to depart for Fenchurch Street on 18 April 2003. *H. C. Casserley/PDS*

SHOEBURYNESS (1): The LT&SR engine shed at Shoeburyness dated back to the opening of the line in 1884. A good number of Stanier three-cylinder tank engines are on shed in this summer 1957 view, while two rakes of assorted coaching stock stand in the adjacent passenger platforms. Although the station was a terminus, a single track continued beyond to serve a large military installation at Pig's Bay.

The simplified passenger terminus is pictured on 16 April 2003, with unit No 357209 forming the 1652 departure to Fenchurch Street. No trace remains of the steam shed, but the single line to Pig's Bay – out of sight to the right of the car park – still sees occasional use at the time of writing. *Frank Church/PDS*

SHOEBURYNESS (2): With its pasted headcode suggesting that it has just worked an excursion train, LMS Class '5MT' 2-6-0 No 42870 runs on to the turntable at Shoeburyness shed on 23 May 1959. This particular engine was allocated to Willesden (1A) at the time and could well have reached LT&SR metals via the Tottenham & Hampstead Joint Line.

Electrification made Shoeburyness shed redundant and the site was quickly cleared for redevelopment. Apart from the Terminal Close street name there is nothing to indicate that a busy steam depot once stood here. The 'present' photograph is dated 16 April 2003. *Frank Church/PDS*

Great Eastern line to Colchester

The Colchester main line was opened by the Eastern Counties Railway in 1843, as part of a route linking London with Norwich and Yarmouth. The tracks were initially 5-foot gauge, but within 18 months they were converted to the standard 4ft 8½in.

The incorporation of the GER in 1862 brought improved standards and shorter journey times between London and Colchester, culminating in a best time of 64 minutes in 1898. Apart from a brief spell before the Second World War, this schedule was not bettered until 1951, when 'Britannia' haulage enabled one service to reach Colchester in 58 minutes. In 2003, the standard non-stop journey time from London to Colchester is 45 minutes.

Major infrastructure improvements in the British Railways era included electrification from London to Shenfield in 1949 and on to Colchester in 1963. However, the main line beyond Colchester was not wired up until 1985. Today the Colchester line is a busy mixed-traffic route, with heavy container traffic to and from Felixstowe complementing the range of fast and slow passenger services.

ILFORD: The LNER operated an intensive steam-hauled service between London and the Essex suburbs. Class 'F4' 2-4-2T No 7578 (later to become British Railways No 67155) enters Ilford station with the 1.23pm from Liverpool Street to Gidea Park on Saturday 11 June 1938. The route between London and Romford had been quadrupled back in the 1890s and its electrification had been proposed as early as 1905.

The electrified service between London and Shenfield finally began in 1949, initially on the 1,500V DC system. The line and its rolling-stock were later converted to 6.25kV AC operation, then 25kV AC. The present generation of Class 315 stock was introduced in 1980. Unit No 315838 approaches Ilford with the 1133 Liverpool Street to Wickford service on 17 April 2003. *H. C. Casserley/PDS*

CHADWELL HEATH: Freight services on the Great Eastern main line are constantly changing as individual traffic flows are won and lost. A distinctive working for many years was the daily sand train from Marks Tey to Mile End, comprising vacuum-braked HJV hopper wagons. Class 31 locomotives Nos 31224 and 31230 pass Chadwell Heath with 8C35, the 1017 departure from Marks Tey, on 18 February 1987.

The sand terminal at Mile End closed shortly after the date of 'past' photograph, and the HJV wagons and Class 31 locomotives were soon also taken out of service. A more recent freight working is 6M16, the 0916 Enterprise train from Harwich to Wembley, pictured here behind Class 66 No 66115 on 15 August 2000. However, the timetables have since changed again and at the time of writing any wagonload traffic from Harwich uses a night-time path. *Both PDS*

ROMFORD: The LT&SR and GER had few points of regular contact, but Romford station on the GER main line was also served by a single-track LT&SR branch from Upminster, terminating in its own bay platform with run-round loop. Recently repainted with 'British Railways' branding, Johnson 0-4-4T No 58038 stands at Romford with the 1.21pm to Upminster on 13 August 1949 – a 'push and pull' working that would not have required use of the run-round loop. On the right are the newly resignalled and electrified tracks of the ex-GER line.

The Romford-Upminster line was nominated for closure in the Beeching Report and its future was placed in doubt again in the 1970s, with the Greater London Council proposing conversion to a busway. However, it survived and was even electrified in 1986 to remove an awkward pocket of diesel operation. Still looking isolated from the main ex-GER station, the Upminster platform is pictured between trains on 17 April 2003, while unit No 321356 passes by on the main line. *H. C. Casserley/PDS*

SHENFIELD: Large-scale residential development in and around Brentwood prompted the LNER to choose Shenfield as the terminus for its suburban electrification project, delayed by the Second World War but successfully inaugurated in 1949. Main-line trains remained steam-hauled until the arrival of diesels in the late 1950s. Class 'B17' No 61672 passes Shenfield with the 2.50pm Clacton to Liverpool Street train on 23 July 1955.

Class 321 units took over from first-generation electric stock on the Southend line in 1988. Unit No 321332 departs from Shenfield with the 1100 Liverpool Street to Southend service on 16 April 2003. *Hugh Ballantyne/PDS*

CHELMSFORD, Essex's county town, became an important stopping place on the London-Norwich main line, but the station never gained junction status and only had two through platforms. LNER Class 'B1' 4-6-0 No 1119, shortly to become British Railways No 61119, enters Chelmsford with the 2.38pm Lowestoft-Liverpool Street express on 26 June 1948. The 'B1s' were a successful mixed-traffic design and a total of 410 entered service between 1943 and 1952.

Electrification, initially at 1,500V DC, was extended to Chelmsford in 1956. This brought a huge increase in passenger traffic and Chelmsford station was substantially modernised at street level. The electrification was later converted to 6.25kV AC, and finally to 25kV AC. With the lift tower dominating the up platform, the present facilities are pictured on 15 April 2003, with Anglia Railways Class 86 No 86230 propelling the 1330 London to Norwich train. *H. C. Casserley/PDS*

WITHAM: BR Standard 'Britannia' 4-6-2 locomotives took over Norwich line expresses in July 1951, bringing the shortest journey time between Colchester and London down to 58 minutes. No 70012 *John of Gaunt* calls at Witham with the 1.45pm Norwich to Liverpool Street service on 21 March 1959. By this time many of the Norwich expresses were diesel-hauled, but Norwich Thorpe shed retained a substantial allocation of 'Britannias'. Just visible under the shadow of the raised booking hall on the left is a diesel railbus for the Braintree line.

On 15 April 2003 No 86230 calls at Witham with the 1600 Norwich to Liverpool Street train, while unit No 321448 waits to cross over on to the main line with the 1658 service from Braintree to Liverpool Street. *Michael Mensing/PDS*

KELVEDON (MAIN LINE): Kelvedon was an important source of traffic in its own right, quite apart from being the junction station for the Kelvedon, Tiptree & Tollesbury Pier Light Railway. With the steeply graded spur to the Tollesbury branch curving away to the right, an up train enters Kelvedon station on 27 March 1937, headed by Class 'B12' 4-6-0 No 8541.

Kelvedon lost its junction status in 1962 and goods facilities were withdrawn in 1964. The up platform has also been extended, so it is difficult to imagine the branch connection having existed. Calling to pick up City commuters on 14 April 2003 is First Great Eastern unit No 321332, forming the 0718 service from Harwich Town to Liverpool Street. *R. M. Casserley collection/PDS*

MARKS TEY (MAIN LINE): With yellow warning panels not yet imposed, English Electric Type 4 (later Class 40) No D204 passes Marks Tey with the 2.45pm train from Norwich to Liverpool Street on 21 March 1959. The first few EE Type 4s began their working lives on the Great Eastern section, before transfer to the London Midland Region in the 1960s.

The Class 40s on Norwich expresses gave way to Classes 37 and 47, until electric traction took over in 1985. No D204 became 40004 and spent most of its life working from Longsight until withdrawal in the early 1980s. Representing the modern scene, Class 86 No 86234 arrives at Marks Tey with the 1600 Norwich to Liverpool Street train on 14 April 2003. *Michael Mensing/PDS*

COLCHESTER (1): The Eastern Counties Railway built its Colchester station a mile north of the town centre, in order to avoid awkward gradients and to take advantage of cheaper land. The line curved sharply through the station, which led to an irksome 40mph speed restriction for through trains. Approaching Colchester with a down express on 6 September 1947 is LNER Class 'B17' 4-6-0 No 1658 *The Essex Regiment*. On the right is the tranship shed, and behind the train would have been the goods sorting sidings for Colchester.

The curvature on the approach to Colchester was eased during remodelling work in the late 1950s, in readiness for the start of through electric services in 1962. The 0900 London to Norwich train glides into the station on 14 April 2003, with driving van trailer No 9709 leading the formation and loco No 86221 bringing up the rear. On the right is Colchester diesel depot, which maintained a small allocation of Class 03 shunters until the 1980s.
G. R. Mortimer/PDS

COLCHESTER (2): Plans laid by the LNER to remodel Colchester station were delayed by the Second World War, and the layout of 1894 was to remain in use until the late 1950s. Class 'B12' 4-6-0 No 61575 has just arrived in the main down platform with the 8.31am train from Cambridge on 12 April 1958 – rather a large locomotive for a small train.

The remodelling eventually completed in 1962 was so comprehensive that there is no precise visual link between the 'past' and 'present' pictures. The through tracks were realigned to allow 90mph running, although this is rarely used these days, and two additional platform tracks were provided to achieve greater operational flexibility. The scheme also included a 1,200-yard dive-under for down Clacton trains to the east of the station. Unit No 321313 departs with the 0915 Liverpool Street to Ipswich service on 14 April 2003. *D. Holmes/PDS*

PARSONS HEATH: Class 'WD' 2-8-0 No 90471 passes Parsons Heath, about 2½ miles east of Colchester station, with an up mixed goods train on 1 July 1950. In the foreground is part of the roof of Parsons Heath signal box, one of the many small examples that were to be closed and removed before electrification. No 90471 was one of a class of more than 700 'Austerity' 2-8-0s built for the Ministry of Supply during the Second World War and purchased by British Railways in 1948.

Parsons Heath is now a featureless location, with undergrowth obscuring the course of the up and down refuge sidings. A trio of electric locomotives, headed by Class 86 No 86604 in Freightliner green livery, heads the 1044 Ipswich to Trafford Park Freightliner service on 14 April 2003. *G. R. Mortimer/PDS*

Great Eastern branches to the coast

WICKFORD station was conceived as a junction right from the start, with the GER inaugurating its services to both Southend and Southminster in 1889. The two branches were intended to open up large areas of 'New Essex' and, in the case of Southend, to provide competition for the LT&SR. Class 'B12' 4-6-0 No 61576 calls at Wickford with the 12.10pm Shenfield to Southend train on 19 March 1955.

The 'present' photograph of 16 April 2003 shows little evidence of change in the station track layout since the 1950s. Even the Victorian footbridge remains in use, albeit disfigured by a modern parapet, as unit No 321340 arrives with the 1300 Liverpool Street to Southend Victoria service. Stabled in the up-side bay is a second Class 321 unit that will form a peak-hour working to Southminster, supplementing the hourly service of through trains from London. *H. C. Casserley/PDS*

SOUTHEND VICTORIA (1): The GER station at Southend, later known as Southend Victoria, is pictured in pre-Grouping days, with a typical selection of non-motorised road transport in the forecourt. Southend owed its phenomenal growth in the late 19th century largely to the coming of the railways – 50 years earlier it was merely the 'south end' of the village of Prittlewell.

The GER station building remains largely intact to this day, as seen on 16 April 2003. The building sports two prominent examples of the BR double-arrow sign, wisely retained in spite of privatisation as an instantly recognisable railway symbol. *Lens of Sutton/PDS*

SOUTHEND VICTORIA (2): Despite its proximity to London and limited range of services, Southend Victoria developed the feel – and the name – of a main-line terminus. Awaiting departure with a local train to Shenfield in the mid-1950s is Class 'B1' 4-6-0 No 61360, its 30D shed plate showing that it was allocated to Southend Victoria depot.

Electrification reached Southend Victoria in 1956, and the improvement for passengers was matched by new freight facilities including a mechanised coal concentration depot. Today only the passenger traffic remains, with a 20-minute-interval off-peak service enhanced by rush-hour extras. Unit No 321313 awaits departure with the 1830 service to Liverpool Street on 16 April 2003. *Stephen Summerson/PDS*

WOODHAM FERRERS: The Southminster branch was one of the first in the country to go over to diesel multiple unit operation. A Derby lightweight two-car unit, numbered in the E79xxx series, stands in the down platform at Woodham Ferrers on 17 August 1956, just before the start of regular diesel services.

The growth of commuter traffic from towns such as Woodham Ferrers and Burnham-on-Crouch after the Second World War saved the Southminster branch from the threat of closure, but the intermediate stations lost their goods facilities in 1965, and only Fambridge retained its passing loop. On the positive side, BR electrified the branch in 1986 and extended the platforms at Woodham and Southminster to take 12-coach trains. The 'present' photograph is dated 16 April 2003. *Frank Church/PDS*

SOUTHMINSTER (1): Class 'B12' 4-6-0 No 61549 stands at Southminster with the 1.20pm train to Shenfield on 2 April 1955. The survivors of this locomotive class – a 1932 Gresley rebuild of a GER design from 1911 – were scattered between half a dozen East Anglian sheds at that time, this particular example being allocated to Stratford. The signal box dated back to the opening of the line in 1889 and contained a McKenzie & Holland frame with 36 levers.

The railway infrastructure at Southminster has shrunk dramatically, with just a single track and platform sufficing for the hourly passenger service, as seen on 16 April 2003; however, behind the photographer lies an active freight terminal, dispatching spent nuclear fuel rods from Bradwell power station. At the time of writing, Direct Rail Services operates a weekly flask train, running in the path of an off-peak passenger service that is advertised as running 'Thursdays excepted' – a puzzle for the uninitiated! *R. M. Casserley/PDS*

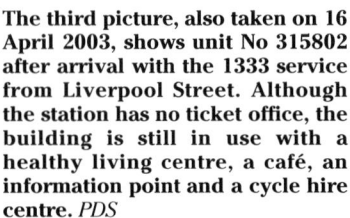

The third picture, also taken on 16 April 2003, shows unit No 315802 after arrival with the 1333 service from Liverpool Street. Although the station has no ticket office, the building is still in use with a healthy living centre, a café, an information point and a cycle hire centre. *PDS*

SOUTHMINSTER (2): This view from the buffer stops shows a Derby lightweight diesel unit, Nos E79252 and E79036, just after arrival with the 10.16am service from Wickford on 15 December 1956. The photographer recalls that the roofless loco shed on the left still displayed a notice to staff dating from GER days.

The simplified terminus is pictured on 16 April 2003, the platform having been lengthened to take 12-coach electric trains. The Derby lightweight '79xxx' diesel units illustrated in the 'past' photograph are almost as distant a memory as the steam locomotives that they replaced – all had been withdrawn by 1970. But they foreshadowed one of the biggest railway changes of the 20th century: the change from locomotive haulage to unit train operation. *Michael Covey-Crump/PDS*

WICKHAM BISHOPS (1): Class 'F5' 2-4-2T No 67195 calls at Wickham Bishops with the 2.24pm Witham to Maldon train on Sunday 4 August 1957. The single-faced platform between the tracks was an unusual feature of this location, with little evidence of change since GER days.

Essex County Council purchased some parts of the Maldon branch in the 1980s, intending to turn the trackbed into a new footpath and cycleway, while other sections of the line, including Wickham Bishops station, have passed into private ownership. In the 'present' photograph, dated 15 April 2003, springtime foliage is about to obscure the view of the restored station building and platform. *G. R. Mortimer/PDS*

WICKHAM BISHOPS (2): Class 'J15' 0-6-0 No 65445 crosses the unique wooden trestle bridge over the River Blackwater with a train bound for Witham on 12 May 1958; this was just four months before diesel railbuses took over regular services on the Maldon branch.

Neither the railbuses, nor the diesel multiple units that followed them in 1963, were able to save the Maldon branch from closure, and the last scheduled passenger train between Witham and Maldon ran in September 1964. Today much of the route is still traceable, and the trestle bridge, seen on 15 April 2003, has been scheduled as an ancient monument. *Frank Church/PDS*

MALDON EAST (1): In its railway heyday, Maldon was the meeting place of branch lines from Witham and Woodham Ferrers, converging at Maldon East station. However, the Woodham Ferrers link lost its passenger service as early as 1939, and by the 1950s all goods as well as passenger traffic was routed via Witham. The size of Maldon East goods shed is an indication of the heavy traffic once generated by local industry, trade and agriculture. Among the sources of freight in GER days were maltings, granaries, market gardening, fruit-growing and even a steel roller mill. Passenger traffic was less impressive, but did include large numbers of day-trippers at summer weekends. On 12 May 1958 venerable Class 'J15' 0-6-0 No 65445 prepares to leave the terminus with a Witham train.

Recent industrial development precludes an exact repeat of the 1958 view, but the more northerly vantage point chosen on 15 April 2003 shows the enormity of the surviving goods shed.

The third picture, taken on the same date, illustrates the well-kept frontage of the former Maldon East station, nearly four decades after its closure. *Frank Church/PDS (2)*

MALDON EAST (2): British Thomson-Houston (BTH) Type 1 No D8220 approaches Maldon East with the 3.41pm service from Witham on 6 August 1960; the Type 1 was deputising for the usual railcar because of carnival traffic. The 44 BTH Type 1s were used mainly on local freight workings on ex-GER routes and all were withdrawn by 1971.

The same location on 15 April 2003 is occupied by the A414 trunk road, which continues towards Chelmsford on the trackbed of the former Woodham Ferrers line. *Frank Church/PDS*

KELVEDON (TOLLESBURY BRANCH): A Light Railway Order of 1901 gave consent for the building of the 10-mile branch from Kelvedon to Tollesbury Pier. Passenger services commenced between Kelvedon and Tollesbury in 1904 and the extension to Tollesbury Pier opened in 1907. Although the branch was worked by the GER from the start, trains on the Light Railway used a separate low-level terminus at Kelvedon, linked to the main-line station by a single-track incline for stock movements and a ramp for pedestrians. The Light Railway terminus and engine shed are pictured on 23 April 1951, just two weeks before the end of regular passenger services.

No trace remains today of the low-level station at Kelvedon, but a view of the modernised main-line station has been opened up. A Class 312 unit calls with the 0718 Ipswich to Liverpool Street service on 14 April 2003. *R. M. Casserley collection/PDS*

TIPTREE was the principal intermediate station between Kelvedon and Tollesbury. The goods yard handled traffic for the local jam factory, which boasted its own internal railway system. There was also seasonal fruit and vegetable traffic. The surprisingly well-kept station platform is pictured on 29 July 1958, seven years after the end of passenger services but with pick-up goods traffic destined to continue as far as Tudwick Road, just south of Tiptree, until 1962.

The careful study of a large-scale map was necessary to find the location of Tiptree station on 14 April 2003. The jam factory is still in operation but has long since placed its reliance on road transport. *Frank Church/PDS*

TOLLESBURY: Although the promoters of the Tollesbury branch had fixed their sights on proposed developments at Tollesbury Pier, including a yachting resort and even a continental packet station, the pier traffic failed to materialise and Tollesbury became the effective terminus of the line in 1921. Ex-LNER Class 'J69' No 8636 (British Railways No 68636) awaits departure from Tollesbury with the 6.37pm to Kelvedon on 26 June 1948. The coaches are No 62261, a six-wheeled 30-foot brake saloon built at Stratford in 1896 and previously used on the Stoke Ferry branch, and No 60461, a 33ft 10½in bogie saloon built in 1884 for the Wisbech & Upwell Tramway.

The section between Tiptree (Tudwick Road sidings) and Tollesbury closed completely in 1951, the victim of increasing road competition. On 14 April 2003 there are few clues to the former existence of a railway at Tollesbury. *H. C. Casserley/PDS*

ST BOTOLPH'S: Given the inconvenient location of Colchester's main line station, it was not surprising when the Tendring Hundred Railway opened a short branch to St Botolph's, a stone's throw from the town centre, in 1866. Despite the awkwardness of run-round movements, the single platform at St Botolph's became a routine calling point for local trains to Clacton and Walton, one of which is pictured on 17 April 1949. By this time St Botolph's had also become an important centre for parcels and freight traffic.

St Botolph's station was extensively refurbished in 1991 and renamed Colchester Town to reflect its central location. Slick operation enables an hourly service between Colchester and Walton-on-the-Naze to call at the platform in each direction, together with an hourly terminating train to and from London. Unit No 312703 calls with the 1020 from Walton-on-the-Naze to Colchester on 14 April 2003. *T. J. Edgington/PDS*

BRIGHTLINGSEA (1): The 5-mile branch from Wivenhoe to Brightlingsea opened in 1866. It was worked by the GER from the start and bought outright by that company in 1893. Although Brightlingsea flourished as a yachting centre and produced a thriving trade in oysters, it was overshadowed as a seaside resort by Clacton and its local population stagnated. The terminus lost its signal box as early as 1922 and the branch nearly closed in January 1953 following severe storm damage. However, repairs were made and services restarted in December of the same year. This mid-1950s scene depicts Class 'J15' 0-6-0 No 65432 waiting to leave Brightlingsea with a Wivenhoe train.

The reprieve turned out to be short-lived. The former station site is pictured on 14 April 2003, with only the 'Railway Tavern' in the middle of the picture recalling the long-lost branch line. *Stephen Summerson/PDS*

BRIGHTLINGSEA (2): Diesel multiple units arrived on the Brightlingsea branch in 1957, bringing an improved service to and from Colchester. An early Metropolitan-Cammell unit stands beside the neat and tidy gas-lit platform on 19 July 1958. Goods trains on the branch were to remain steam-hauled until 1960.

By 1963 fewer than 600 people were using the line each day, and two-thirds of those were concentrated on six of the 30 or so trains. Complete closure took place in June 1964, with passengers being offered a bus connection from Alresford and freight to be delivered by road from Colchester. Today the Brightlingsea Community Centre occupies part of the station site, as seen on 14 April 2003. *Frank Church/PDS*

THORPE-LE-SOKEN: Until recent times many trains conveyed Clacton and Walton portions that divided and combined at Thorpe-le-Soken, giving the station rather more importance than its rural location might otherwise have justified. Class 'B2' 4-6-0 No 61644 attaches Walton coaches to the 4.20 Clacton-Colchester service on 17 April 1949.

British Railways decided to electrify the Clacton and Walton lines in the 1950s, and it was chosen as a testing ground for the new 25kV AC system, which would soon become the standard form of overhead electrification in Britain. With the 1950s gantry and concrete footbridge looking distinctly dated, unit No 312717 calls at Thorpe-le-Soken with the 1520 stopping service from Walton-on-the-Naze on 14 April 2003. Track alterations in 1989 reduced the station to one island platform, with both remaining tracks signalled for bi-directional running. *T. J. Edgington/PDS*

WALTON-ON-THE-NAZE: The Tendring Hundred Railway reached Walton in 1867, some 15 years before the opening of the neighbouring branch to Clacton. Still displaying its LNER number and branding, Class 'F6' 2-4-2T No 7220 stands at Walton ready to haul the 4.17pm departure to Colchester on 17 April 1949. The turntable of Walton engine shed can be seen on the left.

The remaining platform at Walton is pictured on 14 April 2003. Despite its forlorn appearance, the station supports an hourly service to and from Colchester. The houses on the far left provide a clear link between the two photographs. *T. J. Edgington/PDS*

CLACTON-ON-SEA: The opening of the 4½-mile branch from Thorpe-le-Soken to Clacton in 1882 enabled the GER to tap the growing market for summertime trips to the seaside, as well as encouraging the start of commuter settlement in the area. The traffic soon outgrew existing facilities and in 1929 the LNER built a new station for Clacton, followed by the doubling of the track from Thorpe-le-Soken in 1941. The station throat is pictured on 7 July 1956, with ex-LT&SR 4-4-2T No 41949 ready to work the 6.10pm to Colchester and a long rake of excursion stock in one of the carriage sidings.

The GER signal box of 1891 still controls the station area today, with searchlight signals dating from the late 1950s – once commonplace on ex-GER lines but now mostly ousted by standard four-aspect signals. The unusually complex track layout by today's standards is pictured on 14 April 2003. *H. C. Casserley/PDS*

WRABNESS: The ancient port of Harwich was an early target for 19th-century railway promoters, and the 11-mile branch from Manningtree opened under Eastern Counties Railway management in 1854. The small intermediate station at Wrabness retained its original station buildings and signal box until recent times. In the first picture Class 31 No 31184 disturbs the peace with the 2008 Speedlink service from Mossend to Parkeston on 8 April 1983, the consist including a container for Parkeston Quay Freightliner terminal as well as wagonload traffic for the Dunkerque ferry.

The Harwich branch was resignalled and electrified in 1986 and Wrabness became an unstaffed halt. Unit No 321304 calls with the 1246 Manningtree to Harwich Town service on 14 April 2003. *Both PDS*

Perhaps the one attractive feature of Wrabness station today is this mural on the down platform – a cross-section of the line's regular passengers? *PDS*

PARKESTON QUAY owes its existence as a port to the Great Eastern Railway, and was even named after the company's chairman, Mr Charles Parkes. In the early years of the 20th century the quay was handling regular sailings to the Netherlands, Germany, Denmark and Sweden, and the railway supplemented the normal branch passenger service with luxurious boat trains such as the 'Continental Express' introduced in 1904 and the 'Hook Continental' from 1927. With the Great Eastern Hotel dominating the scene, Class 'B12' 4-6-0 No 61570 enters the station with the 10.15am Ipswich to Harwich Town train on 29 August 1948. BR built a new passenger terminal at Parkeston Quay in 1972, further enhancements were carried out in 1984, and the station was renamed Harwich International Port in 1995. Calling at the new platform 2 on 14 April 2003 is unit No 321304, forming the 1346 stopping service from Manningtree to Harwich Town. A plaque on the station platform informs today's passengers of the origins of Parkeston Quay. Despite the rise of air travel, the port still handles substantial passenger and freight traffic. *G. R. Mortimer/PDS*

PARKESTON QUAY
WAS OPENED AS A PASSENGER PORT ON 15th MARCH, 1883 WHEN GREAT EASTERN RAILWAY STEAMERS WERE TRANSFERRED HERE FROM HARWICH CONTINENTAL PIER. THE NEW QUAY WAS NAMED AFTER THE CHAIRMAN OF THE GREAT EASTERN RAILWAY COMPANY, MR CHARLES PARKES.
ERECTED BY THE HARWICH SOCIETY

DOVERCOURT BAY: Rail-borne holidaymakers add a nostalgic touch to this view of Dovercourt Bay station on 9 August 1969, with a Gloucester diesel multiple unit forming the 1303 service from Harwich Town to Manningtree. By this time passenger trains in both directions were using the former up line between Parkeston East and Harwich Town, so the down platform at Dovercourt Bay was out of use. The down line continued to function as a freight siding until the 1990s.

The remaining platform was clean and tidy when visited on 14 April 2003, despite the lack of station staff.
G. R. Mortimer/PDS

HARWICH TOWN station lost much of its importance after the opening of Parkeston Quay in 1883. Class 'N7' 0-6-2T No 69612 is about to complete its run-round manoeuvre in the terminus after arriving with the 1.25pm from Manningtree on 17 April 1949. The sidings curving to the left gave access to the train ferry terminal.

The island platform at Harwich Town was removed to provide enhanced freight facilities, including a terminal for automotive traffic, both import and export. However, my visit of 14 April 2003 found a stout fence erected across the sidings, making any resumption of freight traffic seem unlikely. The remaining passenger platform caters adequately for today's needs. *T. J. Edgington/PDS*

HARWICH TRAIN FERRY TERMINAL: The train ferry service between Harwich and Zeebrugge started in 1927, jointly operated by Great Eastern Train Ferries Limited and its Belgian counterpart. Together with a similar service between Dover and Dunkerque, the train ferry enabled continental wagons to reach all parts of the British railway network, provided of course that they were within the British loading gauge. On 15 August 1970 British Thomson-Houston Type 1 No D8242 unloads wagons at Harwich from the MV *Norfolk* train ferry.

The Harwich-Zeebrugge train ferry doubled its carryings between 1950 and 1960, but after that a decline set in because of the shift towards roll-on/roll-off and container traffic. The operation closed in 1987, with residual traffic transferring to the Dover-Dunkerque route until that too finished in 1995. The derelict linkspan at Harwich is seen on 14 April 2003. *T. J. Edgington/PDS*

Cross-country routes via Braintree, Halstead and Sudbury

WHITE NOTLEY: The line from Witham to Braintree opened in 1848, with intermediate stations at White Notley and Cressing. The single-platform station at White Notley was unusual in having no goods facilities, but a signal box was still required to control the level crossing. Class 'J15' 0-6-0 No 65465 approaches the crossing with a Braintree-bound working on 30 June 1958.

The same scene today is barely recognisable, even allowing for the fact that it was not possible to replicate the exact vantage point. Unit No 321306 calls at the extended and resurfaced platform with the 1132 London Liverpool Street to Braintree service on 15 April 2003. *Frank Church/PDS*

The third view, also dated 15 April 2003, shows that not everything was swept away by modernisation in the 1980s: the wooden cabin seen in the 1958 photograph is still in use today. *PDS*

CRESSING: On 30 June 1958, in the last week before diesel railbuses took over the branch passenger service, Class 'J15' 0-6-0 No 65465 pulls away from Cressing with a Witham to Braintree train. The poster advertises cheap tickets to London available by any train, indicating that commuter traffic had not yet reached this part of rural Essex.

The whole route from Witham to Bishop's Stortford was earmarked for closure in the Beeching Report, but the Witham to Braintree section survived because of large-scale housing developments in the Braintree area. It was electrified in 1977 to remove an isolated pocket of diesel working and to allow the introduction of through commuter trains between Braintree and London. Cressing station is pictured on 15 April 2003, still with its original wooden canopy amid the more functional paraphernalia of the late 20th century. *Frank Church/PDS*

BRAINTREE: The original 1848 terminus at Braintree was replaced by a new through station when the line on to Bishop's Stortford opened in 1869. The earlier facility became a goods depot and was to remain in use as such until the 1980s. Standing in the second station on 13 August 1956 is Class 'F6' 2-4-2T No 67228 with the 3.53pm service from Witham. The GER station building is obscured by the footbridge. By this time Braintree had effectively become a terminus again, following the withdrawal of the Braintree-Bishop's Stortford passenger service in 1952.

Today Braintree supports an hourly-interval off-peak service to and from London, with more trains at peak periods, while a new intermediate station at Braintree Freeport has helped to boost traffic. Unit No 321447 arrives at the terminus with the 1032 service from Liverpool Street on 15 April 2003. *D. Holmes/PDS*

RAYNE: The 18-mile line from Braintree to Bishop's Stortford was never more than a minor cross-country route, and its passenger service of between five and seven trains a day was withdrawn in 1952, although occasional excursions used the line after that. Goods traffic continued into the 1960s, when terminals and services were gradually run down. The disused passenger platform at Rayne is pictured on 9 September 1962, looking towards Braintree.

Rayne closed to goods in 1964 but goods traffic continued to use this portion of the line until the end of the decade. Since then, much of the trackbed between Braintree and Bishop's Stortford has been transformed into a delightful linear country park, named the Flitch Way. The trackless but well-kept station is pictured on 15 April 2003. The station building was sensitively renovated in 1994 for its new role as Visitor Centre and Ranger Base for the Flitch Way, and the former booking hall houses a fascinating exhibition on the former railway and its surroundings. *H. C. Casserley/ PDS (2)*

DUNMOW: Regular passenger services had already finished some four years previously when this busy freight scene at Dunmow was captured on film on 15 August 1956. Class 'J17' 0-6-0 No 65545 stands on the westbound track with a train comprising mainly empty mineral wagons, while a shorter mixed goods working looks ready to depart in the Braintree direction.

The section of line between Dunmow and Felsted closed completely in 1966, placing Dunmow at the end of a 9-mile freight-only branch from Bishop's Stortford; complete closure followed in 1969. Today the trackbed through Dunmow forms part of the A120 road, as seen on 21 April 2003. Recent extensions to the A120 have effectively dashed any hopes of reinstating the Braintree-Bishop's Stortford rail link. *Frank Church/PDS*

MARKS TEY: The 12-mile link from Marks Tey to Sudbury was formally opened in July 1849; initially leased to the Eastern Union Railway, it was not absorbed by the GER until 1898. The junction at Marks Tey faced east in order to allow through running between Sudbury and Colchester. Plans for an additional west-facing junction, thus forming a triangle, were dropped due to lack of funds. Standing in the branch platform at Marks Tey on 30 July 1958 is Class 'J15' 0-6-0 No 65456.

The sidings to the right of the branch platform have become a car park and the branch platform itself has been shortened to accommodate just two coaches. The permanent way is still signalled to allow through running to and from Colchester, but most branch trains at the time of writing terminate at Marks Tey. Unit No 150245 has just arrived with the 0803 service from Sudbury on 14 April 2003. *Frank Church/PDS*

CHAPPEL & WAKES COLNE (1): The line from Marks Tey to Sudbury was reduced to little more than a long siding in the late 1960s, following the withdrawal of local freight services in 1964 and the closure of the Sudbury-Shelford (Cambridge) line in 1967. A Gloucester two-car unit approaches Chappel with the 1128 departure from Sudbury on 13 July 1969, amid a scene of desolation that was all too commonplace on Britain's railways at that time.

In December 1970 the Stour Valley Railway Preservation Society moved into Chappel & Wakes Colne goods yard and began to gather a large collection of railway artefacts and rolling-stock, later opening to the public as the East Anglian Railway Museum. The station footbridge was brought to Chappel from Sudbury and allows access to the museum from the northbound platform, which is still used by First Great Eastern services. The 'present' picture is dated 14 April 2003. *G. R. Mortimer/PDS*

CHAPPEL & WAKES COLNE (2): An elderly Class 'J15' tender engine pulls away from Chappel with a northbound train on 31 July 1958; the bracket signal shows that the route is set for Sudbury, not Halstead. In the goods yard are a low-sided open wagon and a 'Conflat' wagon, both loaded with British Railways 'door-to-door' containers.

On 14 April 2003 unit No 150245 departs from Chappel with the 1743 from Marks Tey to Sudbury. A spur from the Network Rail line caters for occasional stock movements to and from the East Anglian Railway Museum. The original signal box at the north end of the station has been restored, while the museum contains two further pre-Grouping boxes, one of which – Chappel North – is just visible on the centre right. *Frank Church/PDS*

Left Chappel North box is a listed structure that was imported from Mistley in the 1980s, and is the working box on days when the East Anglian Railway Museum runs trains. On the right is the restoration shed, built in the 1980s. *PDS*

73

CHAPPEL JUNCTION: As early as 1846 plans were laid for a 5¾-mile branch from Chappel to the silk-weaving centre of Halstead. However, the plans fell victim to the higher than expected costs of building Chappel Viaduct, but ten years later a separate company, the Colne Valley Railway, managed to resurrect the idea of a Halstead branch. It duly opened to traffic in 1860, from a junction just north of Chappel station. Class 'E4' 2-4-0 No 62785, built by the GER in 1894, approaches the junction with the 5.25pm Sudbury to Marks Tey train on 18 August 1957.

Chappel Junction was removed after the closure of the Colne Valley Railway in 1965. Unit No 150245 passes the overgrown site of the junction with the 1012 departure from Sudbury on 15 April 2003. The 'E4' survived into preservation, first at York and later at Bressingham. *G. R. Mortimer/PDS*

SUDBURY: The pattern of station openings at Sudbury mirrored that at Braintree: the original Sudbury terminus became a goods depot and a new through passenger station was provided when the line was extended westwards in 1865. Both Braintree and Sudbury then became termini again in the 1960s. Arriving at Sudbury with a classic pick-up goods train on 31 July 1958 is Class 'J20' 0-6-0 No 64680. The left-hand tracks led into the goods yard.

After closure of the line to Shelford line in 1967, the remaining Marks Tey-Sudbury section hung on by a thread. Consent for closure was granted in 1972, and it was only local authority intervention that ensured its survival. Economies included the automation of two level crossings and the closure of Sudbury box, while the platform at Sudbury was relocated in 1990 to the down side of the former goods yard to allow the construction of the Kingfisher Leisure Centre. Unit No 150245 arrives with the 0944 service from Marks Tey on 15 April 2003. *Frank Church/PDS*

LAVENHAM: The GER opened its single-track line from Long Melford, on the Sudbury-Haverhill route, to Bury St Edmunds, in 1865. Traffic was never heavy, and the largest of the three intermediate stations was Lavenham, serving a market town with fewer than 2,000 inhabitants. Diesel multiple units were introduced on the line in 1959 but failed to save it from closure. The last passenger train, a diesel-hauled ramblers' excursion, is pictured passing Lavenham on 4 June 1961.

Freight traffic continued to reach Lavenham from the Bury direction until 1965, after which the whole line was abandoned. The site of Lavenham station is now occupied by Silca-Armorex, as seen on 15 April 2003. *A. N. Davenport/PDS*

EARLS COLNE: The first stage of the Colne Valley Railway, between Chappel and Halstead, opened in 1863. The intermediate station at Earls Colne, originally known as Ford Gate, gained new brick station buildings and an extended platform in 1903, as pictured in this postcard from circa 1910. The CVR was unusual in remaining an independent company until 1923.

The railway infrastructure at Earls Colne would have changed little for the best part of half a century after the 'past' photograph, but declining traffic levels after the Second World War led to the inevitable closure to passengers in 1962 and to goods in 1964. The station area is now the Riverside Business Park, with the 1903 building largely intact but partially hidden from view. The 'present' photograph was taken on 15 April 2003. *Tom Middlemass collection/PDS*

HALSTEAD was the principal intermediate station on the CVR, and the location of the CVR's engineering workshops from 1906 until the 1920s. The goods yard handled substantial traffic from local brick factories, as well as supplying the town with coal and other essential commodities. This early 1960s photograph shows British Thomson-Houston Type 1 No D8236 heading east through Halstead with 'The Colne Valley Ramblers' Excursion'.

After the withdrawal of passenger services in 1962, Halstead remained open for goods until complete closure of the line in 1965. A visit to the station site on 15 April 2003 found traces of CVR architecture incorporated into a modern industrial development. *Stanley Creer/PDS*

SIBLE & CASTLE HEDINGHAM: Class 'J15' 0-6-0 No 65464 calls at Sible & Castle Hedingham with a westbound train on 31 July 1958. By this time the arrival of diesels on the CVR was imminent and the end was in sight for the ex-GER 'J15s', although this particular example was to remain in service until 1962.

No trace of the railway remains today at Sible & Castle Hedingham, as confirmed by this view of the former trackbed taken on 28 June 2003. However, in the 1970s an enthusiast group reinstated a section of track a short distance away, to lay the foundations for what is now the thriving Colne Valley Railway, which incorporates the original station building from Sible & Castle Hedingham, as well as signal boxes from Cressing and Wrabness and a varied collection of locomotives and rolling-stock. *Frank Church/PDS*

HAVERHILL SOUTH: The original CVR terminus at Haverhill saw little use by passenger trains and became a goods-only location as early as 1924, shortly after the CVR lost its independence to become part of the LNER. But Haverhill South, as it became known, was to enjoy a long life as a goods depot, finally closing, together with the rest of the CVR, in 1965. The well-kept fan of sidings is pictured on 27 May 1957, with coal being bagged into hundredweight sacks and loaded into a lorry.

Much of the approach to Haverhill South is now buried under an industrial estate, but the former station area was still awaiting development when visited on 28 June 2003. *R. M. Casserley/PDS*

HAVERHILL NORTH: Two years after the Colne Valley Railway established its terminus on the south side of the town, the GER opened a separate through station on its Sudbury to Shelford (Cambridge) line. Thereafter, most CVR trains used the GER station, which became known as Haverhill North. This view shows that station on 19 October 1935, with a train for Marks Tey on the left and Class 'J15' 0-6-0 No 7568 on the right.

No 7568 survived long enough to become British Railways No 65466, while Haverhill North became an unstaffed halt in 1966 and closed completely in the following year. The former station site is pictured on 28 June 2003, with several decades of tree growth obscuring the remains of a platform. The goods shed is now in commercial use. *H. C. Casserley/PDS*

BARTLOW station had separate platforms for the 'main' line from Haverhill and for the Audley End branch. With the station gardens apparently ready for spring planting, Class 'N7' 0-6-2T No 69651 arrives with the 10.17am service from Haverhill on 11 April 1958. The station oil lamps have, unusually, been left in during the day.

The station building was converted into a private house in the 1970s, but the owner retained other railway features including the waiting room and boundary wall on the eastbound platform, making the modern view of 27 March 1993 easily identifiable with the photograph taken 35 years earlier. *D. Holmes/PDS*

Suburban branch lines

ENFIELD TOWN: The Enfield Town branch was opened in 1849 by the Eastern Counties Railway. It was the subject of a very early resignalling scheme, with colour lights coming into use in the 1930s to permit reduced headways for the intensive passenger service. This view of the terminus with lower-quadrant semaphores is dated 12 April 1931 and shows Class 'N7' 0-6-2T No 8005 stabled between duties.

After electrification in 1960, the Enfield branch continued to host an intensive off-peak service of six trains an hour, but the gradual shift towards longer-distance commuting led to a reduction in frequency, and today the off-peak service is half-hourly. The signal box enjoyed a remarkably long life; it eventually controlled the whole of the branch together with much of the Southbury loop, and remained in use until displaced by the West Anglia Route Modernisation project in 2001. The station throat, with the disused box, is pictured on 19 April 2003. *H. C. Casserley/PDS*

CHINGFORD: The GER opened its line to Chingford in 1873 and provided an enlarged station on the present site in 1878. Plans to extend the line through Epping Forest towards Ongar were, however, never realised. Awaiting departure with the 3.40pm from Chingford on 14 September 1957 is Class 'N7' 0-6-2T No 69601, a type that had long associations with local lines out of Liverpool Street.

Steam on the Chingford branch finally gave way to electric operation in 1960, initially using BR standard design AM5 (later Class 305) multiple units. The current generation of sliding-door Class 315 units was introduced in 1980/81, and No 315855, still in 'undercoat' livery in anticipation of West Anglia Great Northern branding, forms the 0807 departure to Liverpool Street on 19 April 2003. *H. C. Casserley/PDS*

GEORGE LANE station opened in 1856 with the Eastern Counties Railway branch to Loughton. The lack of motorised road transport is striking in this view of the frontage in GER days, most probably taken around 1905. A lower-quadrant signal can just be seen above the footbridge.

The station was renamed South Woodford (George Lane) in 1937, later shortened to just South Woodford, and the level crossing was abolished in 1947 at the same time as London Transport took over and electrified the line. Surprisingly for such a small urban station, it retained goods facilities until 1964. The present-day frontage is pictured on 19 April 2003. *Lens of Sutton collection/PDS*

WOODFORD was an intermediate station on the 1856 Loughton branch, but became a junction station in 1903 when the GER opened its 6¼-mile Fairlop loop. Rapid housing development after the First World War created the need for frequent commuter services to and from London Liverpool Street, and in 1935 plans were laid to convert both the 'main line' through Woodford and the Fairlop loop to become extensions of the Central Line. With the days of steam already numbered, LNER Class 'F5' 2-4-2T No 7785 enters the down platform at Woodford on 11 June 1938, prior to working the 4.45pm to Fenchurch Street via Hainault.

The Second World War delayed the Central Line conversion scheme and it was not until 1947 that tube trains reached Woodford. Today the London Underground operates an intensive service on the 'main line' to Epping, but trains on the northern section of the Fairlop loop are relatively infrequent. The 'present' view is dated 19 April 2003. *H. C. Casserley/PDS*

THEYDON BOIS: LNER Class 'F5' 2-4-2T No 7143 enters Theydon Bois station with the 1.17pm Ongar-Loughton train on Saturday 3 April 1937. The rural backdrop is deceptive, as by this time speculative house-building had started to change the face of many villages in the area. However, the line was used by Londoners escaping to the tranquillity of Epping Forest as well as by Essex businessmen commuting to the City.

Since London Transport took over the line in 1949 it has seen three generations of Underground stock. The latest type – 1992 stock built by Adtranz – is represented by this view of a mid-morning Epping to South Acton service on 19 April 2003. At that time services were just getting back to normal after a period of closure following a serious derailment at Chancery Lane. *H. C. Casserley/PDS*

EPPING: The GER opened its extension from Loughton to Epping and Ongar in 1865. The section as far as Epping was converted to Central Line operation in 1949, but it was to be another eight years before electric trains ran through to Ongar, and during that period British Railways operated a steam shuttle service on behalf of London Underground. Ex-GER Class 'F5' 2-4-2T No 67200 takes water at Epping on 9 November 1957 in between push-pull duties on the Ongar line, while a train of pre-1938 Central Line tube stock waits in the adjacent platform.

After 1957, steam continued to reach Epping and Ongar for a time on pick-up goods trains, until these were dieselised, then withdrawn in 1966. Today, since closure of the line to Ongar, both platforms at Epping are used by Central Line services. A train of 1992 stock awaits departure on 19 April 2003. *Michael Covey-Crump/PDS*

NORTH WEALD was the only passing loop on the single-track Ongar extension. An Ongar-bound service comprising experimental 1935 stock pauses for custom on 18 November 1957, in the first week of electric operation. The use of a two-car tube train – compared with trains of between six and eight cars elsewhere on the Underground – is a reminder that this rural outpost never became successfully integrated into the London Transport network.

The loop and signal box at North Weald were taken out of use in 1976 as London Underground tried to reduce its losses on the Ongar branch. However, the only effective cost-cutting measure was to be the complete closure of the line in 1994. Happily, North Weald signal box has been restored and the GER station house is still inhabited, while the platform looks uncannily ready to receive its next trainload of passengers. The 'present' scene is dated 16 April 2003. *Frank Church/PDS*

ONGAR was a classic branch terminus, its single-platform passenger station flanked on one side by a goods yard and on the other by a diminutive engine shed. Possible extensions from Ongar to Dunmow or Chelmsford were mooted by the GER but never acted upon. Class 'F5' 2-4-2T No 7144 waits to leave the terminus with the 3.40pm train to Liverpool Street on 11 June 1938.

London Transport first proposed closing the Ongar line in 1970, and it was only the offer of a subsidy from Essex County Council that kept a reduced service going. But the little-used intermediate station at Blake Hall closed in 1981 and the remaining service was then reduced to peak hours only. The inevitable closure of the branch took place in September 1994. Today, Ongar station is the base for an interesting collection of British and Finnish motive power owned by the Epping Ongar Railway, still hoping to restore a train service on the branch. The station is pictured on 15 April 2003. *H. C. Casserley/PDS*

Great Eastern line to Cambridge and branches

The line from Stratford to Bishop's Stortford was opened in stages between 1840 and 1842 by the Northern & Eastern Railway. It was originally built to 5-foot gauge, but was converted to the standard 4ft 8½in gauge when taken over by the Eastern Counties Railway in 1844. The continuation from Bishop's Stortford to Cambridge and Norwich opened in 1845.

Although the line carried some through trains between London and Norwich until recent times, its importance declined after the opening of the route via Ipswich in 1849. Even the London to Cambridge section suffered through competition from the GNR line via Hitchin.

Today, with modern electric trains running at frequent intervals, the route carries heavy London-bound commuter traffic from towns on the Essex/Hertfordshire border and a share of the through traffic between Cambridge and London, plus increasing airline business to and from Stansted.

NORTHUMBERLAND PARK: The Lea Valley line between Clapton Junction and Cheshunt Junction was excluded from the 1960 Chingford/Enfield/Hertford electrification scheme because it carried mainly long-distance passenger and freight traffic. Ex-LNER Class 'K1' 2-6-0 No 62039 passes Northumberland Park with the 12.45pm Saturdays-only train from Cambridge to London Liverpool Street on 2 July 1960; at that time the tracks to the right of the station would have been with busy with freight traffic to and from Temple Mills yard.

Mechanical signalling on the Lea Valley line lasted until 1969, when BR finally electrified the 'missing link' between Clapton and Cheshunt. The replacement colour light signalling at Northumberland Park was then controlled from Temple Mills West Junction. However, further modernisation came in 2002 when Liverpool Street Signal Control Centre took over the line as part of the massive West Anglia Route Modernisation project. Unit No 317660 approaches the now unstaffed station with the 1344 from Bishop's Stortford to London Liverpool Street on 19 April 2003. *H. C. Casserley/PDS*

HARLOW MILL: British Railways introduced 'Britannia' haulage to its London-Cambridge-King's Lynn expresses in the early 1950s, enabling faster schedules on this key route. No 70037 *Hereward the Wake* speeds through Harlow station with the 4.45pm Cambridge-Liverpool Street express of 2 June 1956.

Harlow station was renamed Harlow Mill in 1960, at the same time as British Railways opened a new Harlow Town station just under 2 miles further west. The former Great Eastern signal box gave way to a new power box, although by today's standards it controlled only a short section of route; it in turn closed in October 2003 as part of the final stage of the West Anglia route upgrade. West Anglia Great Northern unit No 317670 calls with the 1612 service from Bishop's Stortford to London Liverpool Street on 21 April 2003. *H. C. Casserley/PDS*

BISHOP'S STORTFORD: A line-up of stored Class 'L1' 2-6-4 tank engines stands beside Bishop's Stortford station on 17 July 1957, as Class 'B1' 4-6-0 No 61393 calls with a down Cambridge train. By this time, Bishop's Stortford was beginning to generate substantial commuter traffic to London, and the masts and wires of 6.25kV AC electrification were soon to appear.

The station area was remodelled and resignalled as part of the 1960 electrification scheme. Further alterations, including platform lengthening, took place in the late 1980s. Electric working was extended from here to Cambridge in 1987, and the branch to Stansted Airport opened in 1991. BR provided a dedicated fleet of five Class 322 electric units for the London-Stansted shuttles, although they have since been transferred away. One such unit, No 322483, calls at Bishop's Stortford on 26 March 1993. *Stanley Creer/PDS*

ELSENHAM: Before electrification, local services between Bishop's Stortford and Cambridge were in the hands of diesel units. A two-car Cravens unit, Nos E51265 and E54417, passes Elsenham with empty stock working to Bishop's Stortford on 9 April 1983, later to form the 1048 departure to Cambridge.

The line through Elsenham was resignalled shortly after the date of the 'past' photograph. However, the station retains its manual level crossing gates and well-kept wooden platform buildings and canopies, albeit accompanied by modern signage and a digital clock. Unit No 317657 calls with the Sundays-only 1620 Cambridge to Stansted Airport service on 13 April 2003. *Both PDS*

AUDLEY END: Originally named Wenden after the village in which it was situated, Audley End station soon became an important stopping point on the Cambridge line because of its proximity to Saffron Walden. Class 'B1' 4-6-0 No 61042 approaches the down platform with the 2.24pm Liverpool Street to Norwich train on 22 September 1956.

Commuter traffic from Audley End increased rapidly from the 1960s onwards, and today the station enjoys frequent electric services to London and Cambridge. However, the route no longer sees through trains to Norwich and the only locomotive-hauled workings are freight trains. Unit No 317335 forms the 1619 Liverpool Street to Cambridge service on 28 June 2003. The fine building on the up platform, dating back to the opening of the Bishop's Stortford to Brandon line in 1845, is a remarkable survivor. *H. C. Casserley/PDS*

WHITTLESFORD retained its freight facilities long after most other small stations on the Cambridge line, mainly because it handled chemicals traffic to and from the CIBA-Geigy works at Duxford. The yard at neighbouring Great Chesterford survived for the same reason. A Cravens two-car diesel unit, Nos E51261 and E56139, passes a selection of continental tank wagons on the approach to Whittlesford on 5 June 1981. The use of a telephoto lens emphasises the relatively complex track layout at this small country station.

Whittlesford continued to handle some CIBA-Geigy traffic after the Duxford works gained its own rail connection, but this arrangement did not last long. Even the sidings at Duxford closed in the early 1990s following the end of the Speedlink wagonload network. Today the former grain-loading facility at Whittlesford still stands as a reminder of the once thriving goods yard, while the extended platforms and enlarged car park hint at the rise of long-distance commuting from local villages. Unit No 317652 forms the 1634 Cambridge to London Liverpool Street service on 28 June 2003. *Both PDS*

ST MARGARETS became a railway junction when the Buntingford branch opened in 1863, and it was to remain a junction for just over a century, with Buntingford trains using the up-side bay platform. On 16 April 1957 Class 'N7' 0-6-2T No 69653 arrives at St Margarets with the 11.43am Hertford-Liverpool Street train, while on the right No 69634 is backing stock into the bay platform to form the 12.10pm to Buntingford. A large fleet of 'N7s' was allocated to Stratford and Hertford East sheds.

Today it is hard to believe that a junction at St Margarets ever existed. The 0738 Hertford East to Liverpool Street service is about to call at the lengthened up platform on 16 April 2003, formed of units Nos 317336 and 317657. These were built originally for the St Pancras to Bedford line but transferred to other routes when Thameslink opened in 1988. *H. C. Casserley/PDS*

WARE: With electrification apparently complete but not yet in regular use, Class 'L1' 2-6-4T No 67711 pulls away from Ware station with a Hertford East service on the wet morning of 12 November 1960. The section through Ware station had always been a single-track bottleneck, while the lifting level crossing barriers were among the first to be installed on the BR network.

The railway infrastructure at Ware has changed rather less than the surrounding buildings and roads in the last four decades. Unit No 315844 arrives with the 1653 Hertford East to Liverpool Street service on 21 April 2003.
Michael Covey-Crump/PDS

HERTFORD EAST: The Northern & Eastern Railway opened its 7-mile branch from Broxbourne to Hertford in 1843. For its first year of operation it shared the non-standard 5-foot gauge of the N&ER main line to Bishop's Stortford. In 1888 the original Hertford station was replaced by the present terminus, on a site much closer to the town centre. The attractive station building with its covered portico for horse-drawn vehicles is pictured on 27 May 1969.

The changes of the last 25 years have been subtle rather than sweeping, and the station building has been well maintained both internally and externally by BR and its successor, the West Anglia Great Northern Railway. The 'present' scene is dated 21 April 2003. *T. J. Edgington/PDS*

HADHAM was one of six intermediate stations on the 13¾-mile Buntingford branch, opened under GER control in 1863. This was the location of the first passing loop on the branch; others were later provided as traffic volumes grew. This view, dated 2 June 1956, is taken from the rear of the 2.26pm from Buntingford and shows Class 'N7' 0-6-2T No 69685 heading north with the 2.28pm from St Margarets. Somewhat curiously the trap point is not set for the dead-end siding, as it should be!

After closure in 1965, the station site at Hadham remained derelict until colonised in the 1990s by speculative housing development. No trace of the railway's presence remained on 27 March 1993. *H. C. Casserley/PDS*

BRAUGHING: A diesel multiple-unit took over the Buntingford branch passenger service in 1959. This enabled costs to be reduced, but not sufficiently to ensure the line's survival. The loss of through trains to and from London and the cancellation of most off-peak services in 1960 made the line even less attractive to potential commuters, who increasingly chose to drive to railheads such as Ware or Broxbourne. An afternoon train from Buntingford calls at Braughing on 14 November 1964, the last day of passenger services on the branch.

Today Braughing is the best preserved of all the former stations on the Buntingford branch, with both platforms still in position and now forming part of a private garden, as pictured on 21 April 2003. *Michael Covey-Crump/PDS*

BUNTINGFORD: In the last full year of steam-hauled passenger trains on the branch, Class 'N7' 0-6-2T No 69723 stands at Buntingford with a St Margarets train on 13 June 1958. Immediately behind the locomotive is a Southern Railway-design parcels van, by this time a common sight on many parts of the network. A rake of 16-ton mineral wagons stands in the sidings, no doubt having arrived with household coal.

The last goods train left Buntingford in September 1965, ten months after the branch closed to passengers. Most of the station site was redeveloped, but the substantial station house was turned into offices for a local engineering company. It looks strangely incongruous in its residential setting, as recorded on 21 April 2003. *Frank Church/PDS*

HENHAM: The population of Thaxted fell by more than a third between 1851 and 1901, a decline largely brought about by agricultural depression but exacerbated by the lack of a railway. Local interests therefore promoted the 5½-mile Elsenham & Thaxted Light Railway, which opened to traffic in 1913. Despite its 'light railway' status, the Thaxted branch was operated by the GER and passed to the LNER at the 1923 Grouping. A typical scene at Henham, one of the line's intermediate halts, is pictured on 15 August 1936, showing the already antiquated six-wheeled coaches with end-steps, which were to remain in use until 1948. The locomotive is LNER Class 'J69' 0-6-0T No 7193, later to become British Railways No 68600.

The line was so lightly engineered that some sections of it are impossible to trace today except with the help of a large-scale map. This is the site of Henham Halt on 13 April 2003. *Tom Middlemass collection/PDS*

CUTLERS GREEN, another of the intermediate halts on the Thaxted branch, is pictured on 30 June 1951, after the 1.43pm from Elsenham had deposited a few passengers. By this time the 'Farmers' Line', as it was often called, was nearing the end of its short life, with passenger services due to cease in September 1952. The grounded wooden coach body provided typical accommodation for GER halts, not only on the Thaxted branch.

Today Cutlers Green is one of the few locations on the former branch where the trackbed can be readily traced, even though there are no railway structures as such. The present-day scene is pictured on 13 April 2003. *H. C. Casserley/PDS*

THAXTED (1): The terminus at Thaxted lay in a remote rural setting just under a mile away from the village centre. This, coupled with the slow journey times – there was a 25mph speed limit on the branch – and the fact that main-line passengers had to rebook at Elsenham, rendered the operation particularly vulnerable to road competition. A train awaits departure from Thaxted in the last month of operation, September 1952.

Goods trains continued to serve Thaxted until 1953, after which the line and its structures were sold off piecemeal. The station building at Thaxted has survived remarkably unscathed in commercial use, as seen on 13 April 2003. *Michael Covey-Crump/PDS*

THAXTED (2): That such a minor branch line should have had its own engine shed seems extraordinary by modern standards, especially as there was no signalling on the branch and only one locomotive could be in steam at any one time. However, it saved running a tank engine along the line from Bishop's Stortford, and no doubt the crew lived – or lodged – in Thaxted. Class 'J69' 0-6-0T No 68530 stands at Thaxted shed between duties on 30 June 1951. The 'J69s' dated back to the early 1900s, but many examples remained in service on former LNER lines in the 1950s and the last withdrawals did not take place until 1962.

On 13 April 2003, half a century after the railway closed, the engine shed and water tower are still standing, successfully adapted as storage units. *H. C. Casserley/PDS*

AUDLEY END (BRANCH PLATFORM): Operated from the outset by the GER, the independently promoted branch from Audley End to Saffron Walden was opened in 1865, and onwards to Bartlow in the following year. The GER took ownership of the line in 1877, but continued to run it as a country branch, despite its connections with the London-Cambridge line at one end and the Cambridge-Colchester line at the other. A push-pull train for Bartlow awaits departure from the branch platform at Audley End on 16 June 1958, just a couple of weeks before the service was taken over by a diesel railbus. The development of Audley End as a 'park and ride' station seems already to have begun, judging by the car park in the 'vee' between the main and branch platforms.

Today, the car park extends over the former branch trackbed and provides space for several hundred vehicles, full to the brim on weekdays but less so at the weekend, as pictured on Saturday 28 June 2003. The brick shelter that once stood on the branch platform is a curious survival. *Frank Church/PDS*

SAFFRON WALDEN (1): The market town of Saffron Walden generated substantial volumes of rail freight, with industries such as a cement works and maltings adding to the usual mixture of wagonload traffics. The wagons in the yard in this view of 16 June 1958 appear to be carrying mainly coal of different grades, but there are also a high-sided coke wagon, a ventilated van and a 'door-to-door' furniture container. The passenger side is represented by two push-pull sets on the right-hand track.

No recognisable features remain in the view dated 28 June 2003. The former goods yard is occupied by high-density housing and the cutting side is obscured by mature trees. *Frank Church/PDS*

SAFFRON WALDEN (2): Class 'E4' 2-4-0 No 62787 stands coupled to an elderly wooden-bodied coach beside Saffron Walden station on 25 August 1956. The 'E4s' were introduced in 1896 and those that survived into the British Railways era were withdrawn soon after this photograph was taken.

The Saffron Walden line closed to passengers and goods in 1964, the conversion to diesel operation having failed to restore falling traffic levels. A visit in 1993 found the trackbed clearly discernible but the station house derelict and the goods yard partly occupied by a garage. *R. C. Riley/PDS*

A further visit on 28 June 2003 found the station house revitalised as a pair of semi-detached houses, with much of the original detailing extant alongside modern additions such as the valanced canopy. *PDS*

ASHDON HALT was originally the only stopping place apart from Saffron Walden on the 7-mile line between Audley End and Bartlow, although a further halt at Acrow Works was opened in 1957. A single passenger alights from the 9.35am Audley End to Haverhill push-pull train on 14 June 1958, hauled by Class 'N7' 0-6-2T No 69690. This working would have reversed at Bartlow to complete its journey.

The section between Saffron Walden and Bartlow carried very little traffic and its survival until 1964 seems surprising in retrospect. The 'present' scene dated 28 June 2003 shows the overgrown platform at Ashdon with what appears to be the same grounded coach body as in 1958. Both photographs display warnings for visitors not to venture beyond the public footpath! *G. R. Mortimer/PDS*

Great Northern lines

The Great Northern Railway main line from London to Peterborough opened in 1850, offering a more direct alternative to the existing Eastern Counties Railway route via Cambridge and Ely. By the 1860s the GNR was working with the North Eastern and the North British companies to provide through expresses between London and Edinburgh.

Just before the 1923 Grouping the GNR introduced the Gresley 'Pacifics', enabling faster speeds as well as the first non-stop running between London and Newcastle. The design of the 'Pacifics' was gradually refined, culminating in the introduction of Britain's first streamlined train, the 'A4'-hauled 'Silver Jubilee', in 1935.

The outbreak of the Second World War delayed further improvements, and the next major milestone for East Coast Main Line traffic was the arrival of the 'Deltics' in 1961/2. They gave way to High Speed Train (now InterCity 125) sets in the late 1970s, followed by electric InterCity 225 trains from 1989 onwards. A few services are worked by surplus Eurostar sets at the time of writing.

The busy southern stretch of the East Coast Main Line suffered the handicap of double-track bottlenecks at Hadley Wood, Welwyn, Arlesey and Sandy. British Railways started a programme of quadrupling in the 1950s, but the Welwyn bottleneck remains one of the busiest stretches of double-track railway in the country.

NEW BARNET: Gresley streamlined 'A4' 4-6-0 No 4468 *Mallard* approaches New Barnet station with an up express, likely to have been the 11.45am Hull-Kings Cross, on 23 July 1938. This was just a couple of weeks after *Mallard* had broken the world speed record for steam, attaining a speed of just over 126mph on the descent of Stoke Bank and maintaining an average of 120.4mph for an exhilarating 5 miles.

Mallard became British Railways No 60022 and was one of six 'A4s' to pass into preservation. Steam on East Coast expresses gave way to diesel traction in the early 1960s and the first electrics arrived in the late 1980s. But some diesel trains are still required to operate through services to and from non-electrified locations. An InterCity 125 set forms the 0755 Aberdeen-Kings Cross on 28 July 2003. *H. C. Casserley/PDS*

HADLEY WOOD: The two-platform station is pictured on 13 July 1952, with 'A3' Pacific No 60106 *Flying Fox* hauling the 10.00am Sundays-only departure from Kings Cross to Newcastle. Beyond the station is the 384-yard Hadley Wood South Tunnel, one of the reasons why this stretch of the East Coast main line was still only double-track.

The reconstruction of 1955 left no trace of the original Hadley Wood station. The former up and down lines became the up slow and up fast lines respectively, while a new alignment was provided for the down slow and down fast lines; the former down platform became an island platform between the two fast lines. Unit No 317358, carrying the standard Network South East livery of the time, speeds through on the down fast line with the 0950 from Kings Cross to Royston on 26 October 1993. *Brian Morrison/PDS*

POTTERS BAR: Apparently making little impact on the gathering of boy scouts on the up platform, Class 'N2' 0-6-2T No 4758 enters Potters Bar station with the 4.20pm Kings Cross-Hatfield suburban service on 11 August 1945, formed of a 'quad-art' set comprising four coach bodies mounted on five bogies. This batch of 'N2s' had condensing gear and a short chimney to allow them to work over the 'Widened Lines' to Moorgate.

Representing the latest generation of outer suburban stock, West Anglia Great Northern unit No 365520 glides into the down fast platform with the 1515 Kings Cross-Cambridge train on 28 July 2003. Between the taking of the two photographs, the era of Nationalisation has come and gone. *H. C. Casserley/PDS*

WELHAM GREEN: BR provided a fleet of 26 Class 312 units for the Kings Cross outer suburban electrification scheme in 1978. They were based on an early 1960s design and were the last type of slam-door suburban stock built for Britain's national railway system. No 312714 passes the site of the yet-to-be-built Welham Green station with the 1506 Kings Cross-Royston service on 13 April 1986.

Welham Green station opened in September 1986. The grouping of tracks by direction, with the two slow lines on the outside, meant that only two platforms needed to be built at Welham Green, and no alteration to the track layout was necessary. Calling at the up platform on 21 April 2003 is unit No 313027 with an evening train from Welwyn Garden City to Moorgate. *Both PDS*

WELWYN GARDEN CITY (1): The station at Welwyn Garden City was a late addition to the railway network, opening in 1926 to serve the new town conceived by Sir Ebenezer Howard. The passenger facilities comprised two island platforms, while freight customers were provided with a spacious and well-equipped goods yard on the up side of the line. Shunting the yard while working a northbound freight on 15 June 1957 is ex-LNER 'K3' 2-6-0 No 61873.

The goods yard continued to handle occasional wagonload traffic from mainland Europe until the 1970s, and after that the Government provided a Section 8 Freight Facilities Grant to develop a private rail freight facility on the site. However, the new terminal failed to attract any long-term business and has since been fenced off from the main line. The sidings next to the station remain in use for infrastructure traffic and run-round movements, as pictured on 26 October 1993. *Michael Covey-Crump/PDS*

WELWYN GARDEN CITY (2): The Class 55 'Deltics' ushered in a new phase of journey time improvements on the East Coast Main Line, especially after 1968 when BR introduced a new 'fast and frequent' timetable with 'Deltics' hauling trains of only eight coaches. But their heyday turned out to be short: in 1978 the first High Speed Trains arrived, and by January 1982 all 22 'Deltics' had been withdrawn. Heading north through Welwyn Garden City on 31 December 1981 is No 55021 *Argyll & Sutherland Highlander* with the 1005 London Kings Cross-York. This was the last duty for No 55021 and the last day of 'Deltic' haulage on regular service trains.

On 28 July 2003 a Class 91 passes the same spot with the 0830 service from London Kings Cross to Newcastle. Passengers now benefit from air-conditioned stock, but many regret the loss of opening windows. *Both PDS*

WELWYN GARDEN CITY (3): A three-way junction, with branches to Hertford in the east and Dunstable via Luton in the west, was established at Welwyn Garden City even before the opening of the main-line station. Class 'N7' 0-6-2T No 69692 stands at the outer face of the down-side platform on 8 August 1959, forming a local service from Dunstable to Hatfield.

The first stage of the Great Northern electrification scheme, covering the lines from Moorgate to Welwyn Garden City and Hertford North, was inaugurated in 1976, with a fleet of 64 Class 313 electric units covering both routes. A flyover south of Welwyn Garden City enabled inner suburban trains to depart from the down side without conflicting with the main line. On 26 October 1993 unit No 313043 has just arrived with the 1128 service from Moorgate. On the left is the Howard Centre, a shopping centre built partly on railway land and completed in 1990. *Stephen Summerson/PDS*

WELWYN NORTH: New England (35A)-based 'Austerity' 2-8-0 No 90158 heads north through Welwyn North station on 17 April 1954 with a typical unfitted goods train of that era. The rear of the train is passing over the 40-arch Welwyn Viaduct, and the locomotive is about to dive into the first of the two Welwyn Tunnels. This was an expensive line to build!

Welwyn North station has changed less than many others on the GNR main line. It has even retained its lattice footbridge, although a high-topped parapet has been added to conform to modern standards on an electrified railway. Unit No 317336 calls with the 1220 London Kings Cross-Letchworth service on 26 October 1993. Railtrack once aspired to building a second viaduct and pair of tunnels at Welwyn to remove the remaining bottleneck, but what chance now? *Brian Morrison/PDS*

HERTFORD NORTH (1): The GNR Enfield branch was extended to Cuffley in 1910 and, in rudimentary form, to Langley Junction via Hertford in 1918, but it was not until 1924 that the LNER introduced regular passenger services over the Hertford loop. They connected at Hertford North with the earlier GNR branch from Hatfield and Welwyn Garden City. Class 'N7' 0-6-2T No 69695 has just arrived with the 5.7pm from Welwyn Garden City on 9 June 1951.

Today Hertford North is well used by London commuter traffic. Electrification brought an increase in the number of through trains between Hertford and Stevenage, a line that in its early days struggled to justify a passenger service at all. Unit No 317665 departs with the 1730 Stevenage-Kings Cross working on 21 April 2003.
T. J. Edgington/PDS

HERTFORD NORTH (2): Class 'N2' 0-6-2T No 69581 is pictured shortly after leaving Hertford North with a Kings Cross train on 2 July 1953. The rolling-stock appears to be a pair of 'quad-art' sets, each set capable of holding 324 passengers squeezed together in narrow six-a-side compartments. The photographer is standing on the branch from Welwyn Garden City, which by this time was freight-only.

A visit to the same location on 2 August 1993 found several decades of tree growth blocking the view of the Hertford loop bridge. A pleasant footpath now runs along the former Welwyn Garden City line trackbed. *Stanley Creer/PDS*

COLE GREEN: One of the earliest line closures in Hertfordshire was the Welwyn Garden City-Hertford North line, which lost its passenger service in 1951 – some 12 years before the publication of the Beeching Report. An enthusiasts' special, consisting of a Cravens two-car diesel unit, pauses at the former Cole Green station in November 1959.

Through freight traffic over the line ceased in 1962, when the section through Cole Green was abandoned. Rubbish trains continued to operate from Welwyn Garden City to Holwell, just west of Cole Green, until 1966, and a short stub of the former line within Welwyn Garden City, serving the Norton Abrasives factory, remained in use until 1981. The remnants of the down platform at Cole Green are pictured on 2 August 1993. *Kevin Lane collection/PDS*

HITCHIN became a three-way junction in 1857 when the Bedford line was opened to join the existing East Coast Main Line and Cambridge branch. This late-1950s view from the north end of the station platform shows Class 'A3' 4-6-2 No 60062 arriving from the Peterborough direction with an up unfitted goods train – a relatively unusual sight, as the 'A3s' were mainly passenger engines.

The Great Northern electrification scheme reached Hitchin in the late 1970s, by which time the signal boxes and semaphore signals had been swept away. The Bedford line was less fortunate, having closed in 1962. Unit No 317356 approaches the station with the 1005 Peterborough-Kings Cross train on 25 March 1994. Plans to build a flyover to replace the flat crossing appear to have been shelved. *Stephen Summerson/PDS*

THREE COUNTIES: Located just under 4 miles north of Hitchin, Three Counties station closed to passengers as early as 1959, together with neighbouring Arlesey. However, it retained its pre-Grouping signal box into the diesel era, as pictured on 17 September 1974.

Electrification was extended from Hitchin to Huntingdon in 1986, although it was another two years before InterCity services went over to electric operation. The growth of long-distance commuting led to the reopening of Arlesey station in 1988, but Three Counties was less fortunate. The four-track main line is pictured on 21 April 2003, with a new pedestrian bridge in place of the elegant GNR structure, and spike-topped metal fencing installed on the up side. *H. C. Casserley/PDS*

SANDY remained a bottleneck on the East Coast Main Line until the late 1960s. Speeding north through the delightfully well-kept station on 7 August 1961 is Class 'A4' 4-6-2 No 60003 *Andrew K. McCosh*, hauling the 9.40am Kings Cross-Newcastle express. The British Railways Mark I coaches would have been state-of-the-art at that time.

The closure of the cross-country Bedford-Sandy-Cambridge line in 1968 gave BR the opportunity to remodel Sandy station, with four main-line tracks instead of two for the main line and two for the Cambridge route. Unit No 317346 calls with the 1110 service from London Kings Cross to Peterborough on 25 March 1994. The grain silos in the background once produced substantial rail traffic, but this had come to an end with the run-down of wagonload freight in the 1980s. *Michael Mensing/PDS*

LETCHWORTH (1): The Hitchin to Cambridge line gained a new source of traffic with the founding of Letchworth, the world's first Garden City, in 1903. A temporary wooden halt was provided in 1905, goods facilities followed in 1907, and a permanent station was opened in 1913. The population of Letchworth continued to grow after the Second World War and into the diesel era; the neatly maintained frontage is pictured on 9 September 1971.

The 'present' view, taken on 21 April 2003, shows only minor changes. The station has gained exterior lights, a litterbin, an intruder alarm and telephone boxes, while the short-term parking area is more clearly laid out. The 'Garden City' suffix was officially added in 2000. *R. M. Casserley/PDS*

LETCHWORTH (2): The carriage of domestic coal to hundreds of small depots was once a staple business for Britain's railways. During the 1960s BR tried to make the traffic more economic by closing down the smaller depots and serving only larger 'concentration depots', usually with mechanised handling facilities. However, by the 1980s even the concentration depots were facing the axe as the demand for coal fell and the costs of moving it by rail rose. Letchworth was one of the last rail-served coal depots to survive, and one of the few to receive a Freight Facilities Grant to enable it to handle modern air-braked wagons. Class 31 No 31429 shunts HEA hoppers at Letchworth on 23 March 1990 while working the 0325 Temple Mills-Toton train.

Letchworth coal depot finally closed in November 1990. The site is slowly returning to nature, as pictured on **21 April 2003.** *Both PDS*

ROYSTON: The GNR developed the Royston line as a through route between London and Cambridge to compete with the GER line via Bishop's Stortford. After both companies were subsumed into the LNER, London trains continued to run on both routes, with the ex-GNR line gaining five daily 'Cambridge Buffet Expresses' in 1932. A London-bound service passes Royston on 13 June 1958, hauled by a Class 'B1' 4-6-0 locomotive.

Direct trains between London and Cambridge via Royston ceased in 1978 when the Great Northern electrification scheme reached Royston; any through passengers had to use a diesel connecting service from Royston to Cambridge. However, the wires were eventually extended to Cambridge in 1988, and through services were restored. Unit No 317321 forms the 1654 Cambridge-Kings Cross service on 27 July 2003. *Frank Church/PDS*

INDEX OF LOCATIONS

Ashdon 110
Audley End 95, 107

Barking 9
Bartlow 82
Bishop's Stortford 93
Braintree 67
Braughing 101
Brightlingsea 54-55
Buntingford 102

Chadwell Heath 30
Chalkwell 25
Chappel & Wakes Colne 71-73
Chappel Junction 74
Chelmsford 33
Chingford 84
Clacton-on-Sea 58
Colchester 37-39, 53
Cole Green 121
Corringham Light Railway 20-21
Cressing 66
Cutlers Green 104

Dagenham Dock 13
Dovercourt Bay 62
Dunmow 69

Earls Colne 77
Elsenham 94
Enfield Town 83
Epping 88

George Lane (South Woodford) 85

Hadham 100
Hadley Wood 112
Halstead 78

Harlow Mill 92
Harwich Town 63
Harwich train ferry 64
Haverhill 80-81
Henham 103
Hertford East 99
Hertford North 119-120
Hitchin 122

Ilford 29

Kelvedon 35, 50

Lavenham 76
Leigh-on-Sea 24
Letchworth 125-126

Maldon East 48-49
Marks Tey 6, 26, 70

New Barnet 111
North Weald 89
Northumberland Park 91

Ockendon 11
Ongar 90

Parkeston Quay 60-61
Parsons Heath, Colchester 39
Pitsea 23
Potters Bar 113
Purfleet 15

Rainham 14
Rayne 68
Ripple Lane 12
Romford 31
Royston 127

Saffron Walden 108-109

St Botolph's, Colchester 53
St Margarets 97
Sandy 124
Shenfield 32
Shoeburyness 27-28
Sible & Castle Hedingham 79
South Woodford
  see George Lane
Southend Central 26
Southend Victoria 41-42
Southminster 44-45
Stanford-le-Hope 22
Sudbury 75

Thames Haven branch 19
Thaxted 105-106
Theydon Bois 87
Thorpe-le-Soken 56
Three Counties 123
Tilbury East Junction 18
Tilbury Riverside 16-17
Tiptree 51
Tollesbury 52

Upminster 10

Walton-on-the-Naze 57
Ware 98
Welham Green 114
Welwyn Garden City 115-117
Welwyn North 118
White Notley 65
Whittlesford 96
Wickford 40
Wickham Bishops 46-47
Witham 4-5, 34
Woodford 86
Woodham Ferrers 43
Wrabness 59